Exploring
CENTRAL AMERICA, MEXICO,
AND THE CARIBBEAN

Rose Blue and Corinne J. Naden

Chicago, Illinois

© 2004 Raintree

Published by Raintree,
a division of Reed Elsevier, Inc.
Chicago, Illinois

For information, address the publisher:

Raintree
100 N. LaSalle
Suite 1200
Chicago IL 60602

07 06 05 04 03
10 9 8 7 6 5 4 3 2 1

**Library of Congress Cataloging-in-Publication
Data:**

Blue, Rose.
  Exploring Central America, Mexico, and the
Caribbean / Rose Blue and
Corinne J. Naden.
     p. cm. -- (Exploring the Americas)
Includes bibliographical references and index.
  ISBN 0-7398-4952-2 (Library Binding-
hardcover) -- ISBN 1-4109-0334-6 (pbk.)
  1. Central America--Discovery and
exploration--Juvenile literature. 2. Caribbean
Area--Discovery and exploration--Juvenile
literature. 3. Mexico--Discovery and
exploration--Juvenile literature. 4. Explorers--
Central America--History--16th century--
Juvenile literature.5. Explorers--Caribbean
Area--History--16th century--Juvenile literature.
6. Explorers--Mexico--History--16th century--
Juvenile literature. I. Naden, Corinne J. II.
Title. III. Series: Blue, Rose.
Exploring the Americas.
  F1437.B58 2004
  972'.0009'024--dc21
                              2003004045

Acknowledgments
The author and publishers are grateful to the
following for permission to reproduce copyright
material:

Cover photographs by Bettmann/Corbis, (map)
Corbis

pp. 4, 13, 16, 22, 38 North Wind Picture
Archive; p. 6 Archivo Iconografico, S.A./Corbis;
p. 7 Wolfgang Kaehler/Corbis; pp. 8, 14, 23,
30, 34, 46, 55 Hulton Archive/Getty Images;
pp. 10, 12, 35, 48, 58 Bettmann/Corbis; pp. 17,
28, 49, 52, 57 Mary Evans Picture Library; pp.
18, 27 Bradley Smith/Corbis; p. 21 Yann
Arthus-Bertrand/Corbis; p. 25 Gary Braasch/
Corbis; p. 32 Kevin Schafer/Corbis; p. 37
Danny Lehman/Corbis; p. 40 Bob Krist/Corbis;
p. 41 Christie's Images/Corbis; p. 43 Peter M.
Wilson/ Corbis; p. 44 Corbis; pp. 51, 59 Charles
& Josette Lenars/Corbis; p. 54 Jonathan Blair/
Corbis

Photo research by Kathy Creech

Some words are shown in bold,
like **this.** You can find out what they
mean by looking in the glossary.

Contents

Prologue:

Who Found It?

Christopher Columbus opened the doors for a flood of newcomers to the shores of North and South America. He is hailed as the first major explorer to see what Europeans would call the New World. For generations schoolchildren have been taught that "Christopher Columbus discovered America in 1492." But Columbus really did not discover anything. Native American peoples had been thriving in the Americas for perhaps 40,000 years before Columbus arrived. The Aztecs of Mexico and the Incas of Peru had sophisticated societies that amazed Europeans. From South America to far northern Canada, native peoples were here to meet Columbus and those who followed.

Even if there had been no civilizations when Columbus arrived, he was not the first in the Americas. We know that the Viking Leif Ericson reached Newfoundland or New England around the year 1000. So why do we honor Christopher Columbus? We say he is the discoverer of the Americas because he opened a new world to Europe. His four voyages, from 1492 to 1504, unlocked the gates for European exploration and colonization. The gates have never closed. Although the Americas are named for Amerigo Vespucci, who sailed after Columbus, the capital of the United States, Washington, D.C., is called the District of Columbia. There are countless towns, cities, counties, and rivers named for him. So is the Republic of Colombia in South America.

This story of early exploration in Central America, Mexico, and the

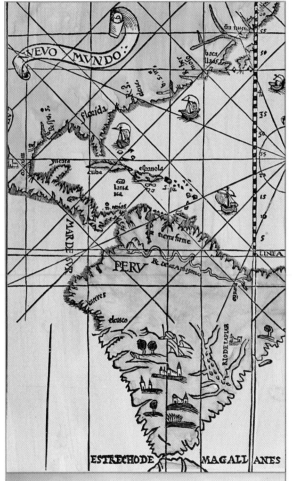

This map of the New World was drawn after Magellan's passage around Cape Horn in 1519.

Caribbean begins with Columbus in 1492 and ends with the conquest of Mexico by Hernan Cortes in the 1520s. In the span of just 30 years, these men would change the world dramatically. This is mainly the story of the conquistadors. They were men such as Cortes, Vasco Nuñez de Balboa, Diego Velazquez de Cuellar, Francisco de Cordoba, Juan de Grijalva, and the Pinzon brothers. Conquistador means "conqueror" in Spanish. These men led the Spanish conquest of Mexico in the 1500s. They were able, efficient, and determined. They were also cruel. Of all the early explorers, the conquistadors in Central and South America probably have the worst reputation for cruelty against the native peoples they met and conquered.

Balboa founded the town of Darien in Colombia, South America. He conducted a series of gold- and slave-hunting expeditions and was the first European to see the Pacific Ocean. Velazquez organized the exploration of Mexico's Yucatan **Peninsula** and was the first Spanish governor of Cuba. Cordoba was the first European to find traces of the Mayan civilization. Grijalva opened the door to Mexico. Cortes won Mexico for Spain and conquered the great Aztec Empire.

These men sailed for their own glory and for the glory of Spain. They also believed that great wealth could be found in this new land. Most of them were ready to carry out their missions by whatever methods possible. The results were often terrible mistreatment of native populations. They helped to write a shameful part of the history of European exploration in the New World.

Despite their methods, the travels of these explorers read like a never-ending adventure story. There is danger at every turn: treacherous waters, impassable jungles, hunger, disease, and death. And always, of course, the excitement of the unknown. Some explorers never made it back home, although most did. For those who did not, some of the men who sailed with them or on different ships returned to tell their stories. Because these men sailed back to Europe and told of their travels, the history of the Americas began to be recorded. Maps were redrawn. Journals were kept. Tales were told. More and more explorers made journeys west. More and more returned with strange and wondrous stories of cities of gold and people very different from themselves. Europeans began to see an enormous unknown world through the eyes of these early explorers.

Explorers do not create and in most cases they do not discover. But they do open doors. They change things. That is why, over the centuries, the story of explorers has remained such a fascinating adventure.

Chapter One
Christopher Columbus
Opening the Doors (1492–1504)

Asked to name just one explorer, almost everyone in the Americas will probably say "Christopher Columbus." He is perhaps the world's most famous **mariner.** Some people thought the United States should have been called the United States of Columbus. In reality he never sailed that far north. He was not even the first European to reach the Americas. However, he is the first historically important European discoverer of the so-called New World. His four voyages from 1492 to 1504 opened the doors for everyone else; for all the exploration, exploitation, and colonization that followed in what became known as the continents of North and South America.

Columbus was an intelligent and imaginative man. His expeditions brought him great honor and riches throughout the European world. Yet his temper and his chaotic rule of the West Indies eventually caused his recall to Spain, where he arrived in chains. Several years later one of the world's greatest explorers died all but forgotten.

A boy of Genoa

Although he sailed in the service of Spain, Christoforo Colombo (1451–1506) was Italian, born in the northern port city of Genoa sometime between August 26 and

This painting shows Christopher Columbus (1451–1506) later in his life.

October 3. At the time, Italy was not yet a nation and Genoa, like Florence and Venice, was called a city-state. A city-state was a country in itself, made up of the main city and its surrounding land.

The details of Columbus's early life are uncertain. Some historians believe that he was actually born in Spain, but Columbus himself said his birthplace was Italy and all the records of his time refer to him as Genoese. Most records say he was the oldest of five children born to Domenico Colombo, a weaver. He might have been of higher birth because later in life he married a noblewoman, which would have been improbable for a commoner at the time. In any case it is unlikely that he received much schooling, although he was well read, had an inquisitive mind, and was aware of the scientific concepts of his day.

Columbus might have gone to sea at about the age of fourteen, not unusual at that time. By the early 1470s, he was a pirate in the service of Rene d'Anjou. In 1476 he fought in a battle off Cape St. Vincent, about 118 miles (190 kilometers) south of Lisbon, Portugal. Ancient geographers regarded this cape as the most western point of Europe. Supposedly his ship caught fire during a sea battle and Columbus swam to shore. Some records indicate that he had been living in Savona in Italy at the time and had joined a convoy of ships that was organized in Genoa and attacked by the Portuguese.

A lighthouse stands at the Cape of St. Vincent in Portugal.

After that, Columbus lived in Lisbon, where there was quite a large Genoese population. The noted mapmaker Bartolome was in Lisbon at the time, as was Columbus's own brother, who was also named Bartolome, or Bartholomew. Bartholomew Columbus was also a cartographer, or mapmaker, and would be a most trusted friend to Columbus all his life. For the next several years, Columbus

Vasco da Gama was one of many great Portuguese mariners.

sailed on Portuguese ships in the Mediterranean and in the Atlantic as far north as England and as far south as present-day Ghana. He may also have made a voyage to Iceland in 1477.

Ferdinand and Isabella

In 1478 Columbus married Felipa Perestrello e Moniz, a noblewoman from one of Portugal's first families. They had a son, Diego, born in 1479 or 1480. For a time they lived on the island of Porto Santo, one of the Madeira Islands that his brother-in-law had inherited. During this period he gained considerable sailing experience in the South Atlantic. When his wife died, sometime between 1481 and 1485, Columbus moved back to Lisbon.

In all the writings that Columbus left behind of his voyages, there is a sense of the dramatic. He felt that he had been chosen for greatness. He saw the wreck of his ship so close to Portugal in 1476 as a divine sign. This was where the great Prince Henry the Navigator (1394–1460) had established an academy. Prince Henry fostered the development of mapmaking techniques and navigational instruments during his lifetime.

Portugal was then the westernmost edge of the known world and mariners just naturally gathered there to talk of the sea and of discovery. Many voyages of exploration had been planned and manned in Lisbon. Columbus had read Marco Polo's account of his journey to China and he probably had heard of a rather fanciful thought by Paolo

Toscanelli of Florence that perhaps the East could be reached by sailing west.

Sometime after his return to Lisbon, Columbus came up with his own idea of sailing west to reach the kingdom of Cipangu (modern Japan), which was thought to be off the eastern coast of Asia. He thought it would be faster and easier than trying to sail around Africa and across the Indian Ocean, which the Portuguese were then trying to do. By Columbus's calculations, his plan would work because of two factors. First, the earth was round (most knowledgeable people of the time believed this, although it had not yet been proven). Second, there was a great distance between Spain and what he called the Indies (meaning Asia). Columbus figured out that the distance between the two was about 3,900 miles (6,275 kilometers). That was a wrong figure for reaching Asia. However, it was the right figure for reaching an unknown continent. This is just about the distance from Spain to the Americas. The great explorer did not know it, but he had figured out how to get to the New World.

Columbus was excited about his plan, which he fully expected to bring him great honor and riches. He presented his idea, called Enterprise of the Indies, to King John II of Portugal in 1484. King John is regarded as one of Portugal's greatest rulers, but was not known for his foresightedness. The king rejected the plan.

Convinced of his destiny, Columbus went elsewhere. The "elsewhere" was Spain. First, he saw the powerful Duque de Medina-Sidonia, but the Duque was not interested either. Then he tried the Conde de Medina Celi, another powerful man. The Conde thought about the plan for a while but decided it was too big an undertaking even for him. He suggested that Columbus see the king and queen of Spain.

King Ferdinand of Aragon and Queen Isabella of Castile had been joint rulers since 1479. Their marriage in 1469 and the joining of the two kingdoms brought about the permanent union of Spain as a country and its beginning as an overseas empire in the Americas.

At first Columbus was handed over to the queen's chief accountant, but finally he was granted an audience with Ferdinand and Isabella in Cordoba in the spring of 1486.

Actually, he had two different audiences with the monarchs, and both times their council of experts rejected his idea. In fact a number of the Spanish nobleman thought the idea was ridiculous and said so. But the king and queen set up the Talavera Commission to study the matter, which it did for about four years. Some of the delay was caused by Columbus himself. He was sometimes vague about his plans and unable to describe them in much detail.

While Columbus waited to hear from the commission, he kept trying to interest others in his idea. Bartholomew tried without success to interest England and France. Columbus himself went back to

Columbus meets with Queen Isabella.

Portugal to see the king. However, in late 1488 Portuguese navigator Bartolomeu Dias returned safely from a voyage around the Cape of Good Hope at the tip of Africa. Now that Portugal had a passageway to India, the king was even less interested in any new sea route than he was before.

During this long waiting period, mostly in Cordoba, Columbus became involved with Beatriz Enrique de Arana. They had a son, Fernando, who was born in 1488.

In 1490 Columbus must have felt as though the long wait was for nothing. The Talavera Commission voted down his proposal. It said the idea would not work because the earth was larger than Columbus thought and no ship could sail that far. But the adventurer had gained some powerful friends at court, most notably Luis de Santangel, chancellor of the royal household of Aragon, and Prior Juan Perez, the queen's confessor. They might have pressured the monarchs to override the commission, which they did in 1491 in an agreement called the Capitulations. Columbus was even granted his rather outrageous demands: he would be knighted for this undertaking; he would be appointed governor and viceroy of any lands he discovered, as well as named "Admiral of the Ocean Sea" (all these titles to remain in his family forever); and he would also get ten percent of any transactions within his admiralty. Perhaps Ferdinand and Isabella agreed to all these conditions because they thought there was little chance that Columbus would succeed in the venture anyway.

The first voyage: 1492–1493

The first voyage of Christopher Columbus had three goals. The main one was to find a short route to the Indies (the Far East) by sailing west. The second goal was twofold: find gold and convert any native peoples he encountered to Christianity. The third goal was more personal to Columbus. A religious man, he wanted to help organize another Christian Crusade to conquer the Holy Land. The money for this venture would come from his expeditions.

After such a long wait to get started, the preparations for the first voyage were accomplished in a rather speedy fashion for the time. By early August 1492, a crew and all supplies were assembled in the town of Palos. Columbus was in command of three ships. His **flagship** was the three-masted, square-rigged, rather tubby cargo vessel *Marigalante*. It was a rented ship owned by Juan de la Cosa, who was Columbus's first officer. Columbus officially renamed it the *Santa Maria*. It was about 117 feet (36 meters) long and held 40 sailors. The ship was made for hauling cargo, not for exploration. It was not suited for sailing near reefs and in shallow island waters. Therefore it was not as agile in the water as the other two ships, known as **caravels,** which were smaller. The *Pinta* had three masts, carried a crew of 26, and was captained by Martin Alonso Pinzon. The *Nina* had four masts and carried 24, with Martin's brother Vicente Yanez Pinzon as captain. He would prove to be the one of the finest sailors of the era. The ships were armed and Columbus also carried cheap merchandise in case he met Native Americans with whom he could trade for the gold he expected to find. According to rumor, the queen had to sell her jewels to fund the expedition, but the money actually came mainly from an organization called the Santa Hermandad (Holy Brotherhood) and also some from Columbus himself.

At half an hour before sunrise on a Friday morning, August 3, 1492, the small fleet sailed out of the harbor at Palos. Nine days later it reached the Canary Islands where it stayed for a month undergoing repairs to the rudder of the *Pinta* and converting the *Nina* to square rigging for a better sail. On September 6, 1492, the voyage that would change the world was underway.

When the ships finally lost sight of land on September 9, Columbus's test as a sea captain really began. Most of his crew were suspicious of the whole idea in the first place and not at all convinced that Columbus was right. Their mood was not helped by the fact that the crossing took more than 33 days; Columbus had figured on 21. He had used the calculations of the Greek mathematician Ptolemy to figure out the size of the earth, but Ptolemy thought the earth was much smaller than it really is. Of course the speed of sailing vessels varies with the speed of the wind. Columbus's ships probably averaged a little less than four **knots,**

The Pinta *and* Santa Maria *sail toward the New World*

with top speed being about eight knots. Therefore, about 100 miles (161 kilometers) a day would be typical; 200 miles (322 kilometers) a day would be rare. The *Santa Maria* was the slowest of the three ships, the *Pinta* the fastest, but the difference between them was perhaps only about 0.1 knot.

It took all of Columbus's willpower and leadership to prevent a **mutiny** on board as day after day passed without sight of land. Even Columbus had doubts. On a couple of occasions, they thought they sighted land but it proved to be an **illusion** each time.

Even with all the anxiety, Columbus was a keen observer at sea. His journal is full of references to weather conditions and cloud formations. Considering that he was sailing during what is now known as hurricane season in the area, the whole voyage is truly remarkable. Despite the mood of the crew and his own occasional doubts, he put his trust in the compass needle and sailed on.

On about October 7 the crew saw birds overhead. Since the crew was really near **mutiny** at this point, the birds were a welcome sight. So were some green branches floating in the water. Surely land was near. On October 11 Columbus himself thought he saw firelight on the horizon. Sometime after midnight on October 12, 1492, a sailor—said to be Rodrigo de Triana—standing in the prow of the Pinta shouted out "Tierra! Tierra!" He had spotted land ahead. Columbus later claimed that he, not Triana, was the first to spot land because he had seen firelight the night before.

Welcome to America

In the morning Columbus and his officials went ashore carrying the royal banner, which the captain planted in the sand to take possession of the land for Spain. Columbus believed he had reached one of the many islands described by Marco Polo off the coast of Asia. Since that area had been named the Indies, he called the native peoples he saw "Indians." That is the name still often used today for Native Americans. But Columbus was not off the coast of Asia. He had reached what was for him a brand new continent. He planted the Spanish royal flag on an island in the Bahamas in what are now known as the West Indies, the many islands that lie between North and South America. Columbus called the new island San Salvador (Holy Savior); the native peoples called it Guanahani.

The exact island that Columbus saw in 1492 is still open to some debate. It has long been accepted that the first landing was on Watlings Island. However, a 1986 National Geographic Society study concluded that he had landed on Samana Cay. Wherever he was, Columbus thought he was in Asia. After two days on the island trading with the Taino people, including what the Europeans called a "kind of dry leaf" (tobacco), he sailed around the Bahamas

Columbus's brother Bartholomew was an accomplished cartographer in his own right.

DON BARTHOLMEO

in search of gold. Unfortunately any harmony between Europeans and islanders vanished almost immediately when Columbus forced several of the Native Americans to accompany him on this search. They began to view the Europeans as only slightly less dangerous than the cannibals who lived on islands farther south.

None of these islands contained the great wealth Columbus had imagined. So when he learned of a large island that the natives called Colba (Cuba), he thought it must be part of Japan or China. Arriving along the north coast of Cuba on October 28, he spent a month searching for gold.

Native Americans on Watling Island greet Columbus while his shipmates plant a cross on the beach.

When he sent crew members into the interior to what he thought might be the city of the Great Khan (now Beijing, China), they returned instead with the first tobacco plants that Europeans had ever seen. Unknown to Columbus at the time, the strange-looking tobacco plant would become very popular in Europe and would be an even greater source of wealth than gold.

Columbus sailed more than 300 miles (483 kilometers) along the Cuban coast. He made several landings and noted the good harbors. He first heard of the Caribs, a native people who were described by other Native Americans as cannibals. His description of Native Americans in his journals is especially interesting. He characterized them as intelligent, handsome people who could be made to work or be ordered around. This general attitude of the European explorers about native peoples in the Americas made it fairly easy to take the next step to slavery.

Suddenly, on November 21, Martin Pinzon on the *Pinta* left the fleet without permission and sailed away. He sailed to the Great Inagua Island in search of gold. But Columbus had no idea whether his second-in-command had gone back to Spain to steal all the glory or whether he had learned of a new location for gold. In his search for Pinzon, Columbus arrived at the island of Haiti, which he named Española (or Hispaniola), which means "Spanish island." Its beauty reminded him of Spain. He named the site where he landed Mole St. Nicolas because it was December 6, the feast day of the saint.

During his tour of the coastline, Columbus met a young Native American leader who was wearing gold ornaments and was willing to trade. A friendship developed and Columbus invited the leader and other Native Americans aboard the *Santa Maria* for a celebration on Christmas eve 1492. Perhaps there was too much celebrating because the *Santa Maria* ran aground on a coral reef that night and had to be abandoned. The Native Americans helped to transfer supplies to the *Nina*.

Columbus decided that God had intended him to leave an establishment on the island, so he founded Villa de la Navidad, the first European settlement in the Americas. Today it is the site of the small Haitian village of Limonade-Bord-de-Mer. He also left behind 38 Spaniards under the command of Diego de Harana, a relative of his mistress. He also left food, stores, and ammunition for one year.

On January 4, 1493, Columbus sailed from La Navidad on the *Nina* and met up with the *Pinta* days later. Whatever explanations Pinzon gave to his commander, Columbus was furious with him, even threatening to have him hanged. Although the two reconciled, they were never again close friends.

Torn between curiosity for more exploration and a desire to return to Spain with his momentous news, Columbus set sail for Europe on January 16, 1493. Taking a more northerly course, the two ships ran into a raging storm in mid-February and became separated. Columbus was so worried that the ship might go down and no one would ever know of his discovery that he sealed a report in a bottle and tossed it overboard. There is no record of the bottle ever being recovered.

Columbus reached Portugal in early March and was received with full honors by King John II on March 9. Word had already spread of the astounding voyage, and Columbus had sent a report ahead to Queen Isabella. The king suggested that Columbus travel to Spain by land, but he declined and sailed the *Nina* to Palos on March 15. Pinzon arrived soon after but died of exhaustion on March 20.

The reception was tumultuous. Columbus soon received a letter from the king and queen asking him to meet them in Barcelona to prepare for a second voyage. Isabella and Ferdinand were afraid that King John of Portugal, who surely was upset with himself for turning down Columbus, might quickly plan an expedition. Columbus was received by the monarchs in great splendor at the court. He stayed there for three months. The news of his voyage spread quickly throughout Europe. Wealth, honor, and a flow of privileges and awards quickly poured in. He was acknowledged as the master of all navigators and as a **mariner** without equal. He was even given the right to display a castle and a lion (the royal symbol) on his coat of arms. Yet the character of Columbus, which would later cause him trouble, can be seen in his insistence to be the one to receive a princely sum for being the first to sight land in what Europeans now called the New World.

The second voyage:
1493–1496

Preparations began almost immediately for the second voyage and just as quickly ran into trouble. Juan de Fonseca was put in charge of assembling the expedition, but he was a better soldier than an administrator. In addition Fonseca's two assistants, Juan de Soria and Francisco Pinelo, thought Columbus was an upstart and had no intention of treating him like a lord no matter what his new title. As for Columbus, he had no intention of listening to anybody but himself.

Considering the friction and the much larger size of this expedition, the fleet was assembled fairly quickly. This time Columbus commanded 17 ships and 1,500 men, including priests, a doctor, several peasants, and Columbus's brother Giacomo, whom everyone called Diego. The **flagship** was once again the *Santa Maria*, but a much larger version of the original. The main objective on the second voyage, at Columbus's suggestion, was colonization:

Columbus shows a new map to King Ferdinand and Queen Isabella.

to establish a permanent trading colony. Converting the native peoples and seeking gold were secondary. He also intended to explore Cuba more extensively to determine if it was an island or part of the mainland.

The fleet sailed from the Spanish port of Cadiz on September 25, 1493. After a stop at the Canary Islands to load food, water, and live animals for the crossing, Columbus sailed west on October 13. Choosing a southwesterly course that gave him the benefit of the trade winds, he sighted land on November 3. Since it was a Sunday, Columbus named the island he saw Dominica. He did not anchor there but sailed on to the small flat island of Marie-Galante (now part of Guadeloupe). From there he sailed to the large island of Guadeloupe where he first met the fierce Carib people. He continued to St. Martin (modern Nevis), to St. Kitts, and to Puerto Rico. On November 14, he landed at Santa Crux (modern St. Croix in the Virgin Islands). There, a fight ensued between the Spaniards and Caribs, which resulted in one death on each side. Some of the Caribs were captured and eventually taken to Spain as slaves.

Columbus was most anxious to return to La Navidad, the settlement and sailors he had left behind in Haiti. Disaster greeted him on November 27. The settlement was in ruins and the unburied bodies of the Spanish crew were everywhere. There is no record of what happened but it is thought that

Giacomo Columbus, also known as Diego, was a part of his brother's second voyage to the New World.

A few trees now stand on the site of Isabella, a settlement founded by Columbus in what is now the Dominican Republic.

trouble developed between the Spanish and the Arawak people. Columbus ordered the bodies to be buried and also ordered a search for gold in the area in case the crew might have hidden it. None was found.

Looking for a better place to settle, Columbus sailed 75 miles (121 kilometers) east to establish a new colony, which he called Isabella. It became the first European city in the New World. Although the small, shallow bay was not a good location for a trading port, Columbus ordered a main square to be laid out with a church, a "royal palace," and about 200 huts for the settlers. Today, Isabella is a ruined settlement on the northern coast of the Dominican Republic.

Shortly after landing at Isabella, Columbus sent Alonso de Ojeda to the interior mountains in search of gold. He was greatly pleased when Ojeda returned with evidence that gold had indeed been found. In early 1494 Columbus sent Ojeda back to Spain with twelve of his seventeen ships loaded with gold and what he thought were spices. He also sent a report on his findings, including the disaster at La Navidad, and requested more supplies by return voyage.

Trouble and illness

In March, Columbus sailed from Isabella to explore Cibao, part of the island where there were reportedly great amounts of gold. He left his inexperienced brother Diego in charge. There was no gold in Cibao, but Columbus founded the settlement of Santo Tomas and left 56 men to build a fortress. When he returned to Isabella, the settlement was in chaos with friction developing between the priests and the Spanish officers. After appointing a council to help Diego govern, Columbus sailed again on April 24 with three of his remaining five ships, this time to explore Cuba, which he sighted on April 29.

For about six weeks Columbus sailed among the small islands of Cuba's southern coast. After veering southward, he saw the island of Jamaica, which he named Santiago, on May 5. Several days later Columbus sailed back to Cuba determined to find out if it was an island or part of the mainland. On June 13 he reached the southernmost point of Cuba (Cape Cruz) and turned back. He had apparently made up his mind that Cuba was a **peninsula** on the mainland of what he still thought was the Indies, or Asia. He made all of his crew swear an oath—or have their tongues cut out—that Cuba was indeed the mainland.

On his way back to Isabella, Columbus visited Jamaica and was going to Puerto Rico when he fell ill. For some time he had been bothered by **arthritis,** but now he contacted **malaria** and was near

death for a few days. He finally returned to Isabella on September 29 but remained ill for several months. The colony had once again fallen into chaos, but his brother Bartholomew arrived and was put in command. However, the colonists remained discontent with the rule of Columbus and his brothers. Some of the leaders had already left for Spain to take their complaints to the Spanish monarchs.

To add to the trouble, by this time the Arawaks were certain that the arrival of the Spanish meant their own destruction. They tried to drive the intruders off the island. But the Spanish were too strong and their guns too powerful. Columbus sent his brother Diego back to Spain with 500 Native American prisoners, who quickly died of European diseases.

In October 1495 an **emissary** sent by Isabella and Ferdinand to report on the situation found that Columbus had imposed a gold tax on the Native Americans, who were once again at the point of rebellion. Disagreements between Columbus and the **emissary** lasted some five months until Columbus decided to sail home and clear up matters. He left Bartholomew in charge and sailed for Spain on March 10, 1496. As soon as he left, Bartholomew abandoned the colony and established another one on the south side of the island at Santo Domingo.

Columbus returned to Spain on one of two vessels that had been built on the island. These became the first

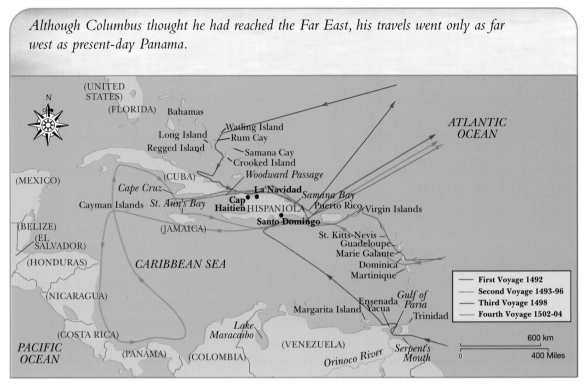

Although Columbus thought he had reached the Far East, his travels went only as far west as present-day Panama.

American ships to arrive in Europe. He dropped anchor at Cadiz on June 11.

The third voyage: 1498–1500

Christopher Columbus did a rather strange thing upon his arrival in Spain in 1496. He entered a monastery for a while and adopted the dress of a Franciscan friar. Perhaps he thought it would protect him from further humiliations at the royal court. Actually he didn't need to worry because Isabella and Ferdinand were not all displeased with him, despite the complaints. Now 45 years old, Columbus still retained the fire and swagger of his earlier days. He had proved to be an efficient, if not very humane, colonizer and soon won over most of his critics. His third voyage was assured. His privileges were confirmed by the king and queen, his material wealth increased, and he was given authorization to populate Espanola with convicts.

This third voyage was smaller than the second, with just 6 ships and 200 men in addition to the crew. Even so, it took some 2 years to get the finances and supplies together. The fleet set sail from Sanlucar, Spain on May 30, 1498. After the usual stop at the Canary Islands in June, Columbus sent 3 of his ships directly to his brother and he sailed southwest with the other 3. He stopped at the Cape Verde Islands and headed west across the Atlantic. On

The Orinoco river flows through the forest in Venezuela.

July 31, Columbus reached the island that he named Trinidad. He landed along its southern shore. When the Spaniards saw Native American women wearing pearl necklaces, there was much excitement because they thought they were in the Far East. However, Columbus figured out that Trinidad was an island, so he quickly sailed into the Gulf of Paria, which separates Trinidad from modern-day Venezuela. He then passed the delta of the Orinoco River.

Seeing the fresh waters flowing into the ocean from the numerous powerful streams of the Orinico made Columbus decide that he was sailing along the coast of a continent. Indeed he was but he still thought it was Asia. Actually it was his first view of the mainland of South America. However, the tidal waves were so powerful and fast that Columbus decided to leave the area as soon as possible. He named the site Boca del Sierpe, or the Serpent's Mouth.

Columbus and some of his officers did go ashore a little farther north. They were the first Europeans since Leif Ericson in the 11th century to step on the

American mainland. Although Columbus would have liked to explore inland to see if he could find a **strait** that would lead to India and the Spice Islands (modern Moluccas), he decided instead to head for Espanola to see what was happening at the settlement. On the way and still taking observations of the North Star, Columbus made numerous calculations and noted that the earth is not a perfect sphere.

Trouble on the island

Bartholomew was at Santo Domingo when Columbus arrived on August 21. Almost immediately Columbus had to put down a rebellion of the colonists. It had been spurred by his brother's heavy-handed reaction to their complaints. This resulted in more complaints against both brothers being sent back to Spain. And things got worse.

By now Isabella and Ferdinand had enough reports of poor administration in the New World to prompt some action. Reluctantly, they decided that their great admiral was a terrible governor. So on August 23, 1500, Francisco de Bobadilla, a trusted old member of the royal household, arrived in Santo Domingo to replace

UGHTER OF THE XARAGUANS AND CAPTURE OF THEIR QUEEN.

Native Americans often received cruel treatment from Columbus and his men.

Columbus if that proved necessary. Upon his arrival he learned that several Spaniards had been hanged on Diego's orders, and five more were awaiting the gallows. Bobadilla ordered the prisoners to be handed over to him, but Diego refused. Seeing the rebellious atmosphere of the colony, Bobadilla announced that he was taking over the governorship. Now Columbus refused, stating that even the king and queen could not deprive him of his position.

Columbus is once again brought before King Ferdinand and Queen Isabella.

Bobadilla immediately had Columbus and his two brothers arrested and put in chains. For a while Columbus thought he was going to be hanged. Instead Bobadilla sent the three men back to Spain. Columbus was treated with respect, but he refused to have his chains taken off. Therefore the great **mariner** arrived in **shackles** in Cadiz in November 1500.

Isabella and Ferdinand were shocked at his treatment and ordered him released immediately. When Columbus and his brothers entered the royal court, he fell on his knees before his patrons.

The king and queen were sympathetic and disapproved of the manner in which Bobadilla had handled the situation, but they also realized that Columbus was not the man to administer Spanish claims in the Americas. After Columbus explained his side of the story and requested restoration of all his titles, including governor, the monarchs issued their decision in September 1501. Columbus and his brothers were absolved of any wrongdoing. Columbus could keep his title of Admiral of the Ocean Sea, but he was no longer governor. Nicolas de Ovando was appointed to administer Santo Domingo. Columbus and his brothers were not permitted to return there.

That seemed like the end of his career as an explorer in the New World. But Columbus, although humbled, was far from defeated. He pointed out to Ferdinand and Isabella that many other explorers were now sailing to the lands he had discovered. They were taking the glory that should be Spain's. Columbus also asked how he could free the Holy Land if he could not go in search of gold to finance such an undertaking.

The monarchs thought that over and finally gave in. Christopher Columbus would have one last voyage as long as he did not go to Santo Domingo.

The fourth voyage: 1502–1504

The last voyage of the man who for centuries has been called the discoverer of America began on May 9, 1502. Columbus sailed from Cadiz with four ships of about 40–50 tons (36–45 metric tons), which he thought best for discovery, and a hand-picked crew of 146 men and boys. That included his

brother Bartholomew in command of one of the ships and his 13-year-old son Fernando. His son Diego, then 21, was left in Spain to represent Columbus at the royal court.

Columbus was indeed correct that since his first voyage, many other mariners had been making discoveries in the Americas. There was even some speculation that perhaps Columbus had not, after all, reached Asia but had landed on a previously unknown continent. However, Columbus clung to his "discovery" and begged Isabella and Ferdinand to let him search for a **strait** that opened into the Indian Ocean. The king and queen agreed but turned down his request once again to stop at Santo Domingo.

On May 25 the fleet left the Canary Islands and on June 15 sighted a previously unknown island that he called Matinino (Martinique in the Lesser Antilles). Then he sailed past Puerto Rico and, despite the ban, headed straight for Santo Domingo. He arrived in the middle of a hurricane. The new governor refused to let him enter the harbor. He rode out the storm in nearby Puerto Hermoso. Columbus would later claim the storm as his reason for requesting entrance to Santo Domingo, but historians are more inclined to think it was his own refusal to bow to authority and his belief that the lands he "discovered" were his own.

Columbus sailed for Jamaica in July and reached modern-day Honduras in

August. Bad weather kept him from exploring the Honduran coast. Fighting a near-**mutiny** by his sea-weary crew, Columbus turned south along the coast of what are now Nicaragua and Costa Rica in Central America, searching for a passage to the west. Ironically, when he reached what is now Panama, he was very near the Pacific Ocean, which is just across the narrow **isthmus** that divides the two oceans. In fact native peoples in the area told him about this isthmus, but Columbus still kept to his dream of the Far East. He decided it was the Malay **Peninsula,** with China to the north and India on the other side across the land strip. Had he not discovered gold at this point, he might have gone on to find that another ocean really was on the other side. Later, Vasco Nuñez de Balboa would cross the isthmus and become the first European to see the Pacific from that side.

Columbus did try to establish a colony in western Panama in February 1503, but he had picked not only one of the rainiest places in the world but one filled with hostile native peoples. He lost one ship and ten members of his crew in a fight. The settlement was abandoned on

The coast of Costa Rica was explored by Columbus on his fourth voyage.

Easter Sunday, April 16, and by mid-May Columbus was on the western end of Cuba. But two of his ships were leaking. It took him a month to sail eastward along the southern coast. After losing another ship in bad weather and with the two remaining ships too damaged to sail on, he landed at St. Ann's Bay, Jamaica, where both ships ran aground on June 23. He was stranded.

Columbus and his 116 or so remaining crew members spent nearly a year in Jamaica. After being stranded for a month, he sent two canoes with 12 men and several Native Americans to seek help from Santo Domingo. But that help did not arrive until late the following spring. By that time only 100 of the crew were still alive. Some reports say Governor Ovando would not send a rescue ship. Columbus battled increasing **arthritis, mutinous** sailors, and hostile Native Americans until he was rescued and reached Santo Domingo in late June 1504.

The last years

In September, a sick and disillusioned Columbus sailed home for the last time. After a stormy crossing, he reached Sanlucar on November 7. So crippled by arthritis that he could barely walk, he retired to his home in Seville. After Queen Isabella died on November 26, he learned that she had not stated in her will, as he had hoped, that he would be "restored in the possession of the Indies." When he was well enough to travel in May 1505, Columbus saw King Ferdinand in Segovia. The king was sympathetic but could not in good conscience restore Columbus as governor of the Indies.

Columbus was well off financially because of the share he received from the gold found in Espanola, but for the rest of his life he tried to get back his promised titles. Discouraged and humiliated, he wrote letter after letter as his health worsened. He died in Valladolid, Spain, on May 20, 1506, at the age of 55. This was two days after he wrote his will, which determined that Diego would inherit most of his fortune. Ironically, few noticed the death of Christopher Columbus. People were too excited by the voyages of Amerigo Vespucci, who correctly declared that Columbus had found what Europeans were calling a New World. Did Columbus himself ever realize where he had really landed? Some experts say a letter written in 1500 in which he talks of his voyages as giving Spain a "second world" is an indication that he finally realized he had stepped on another continent. But no one knows for sure.

Columbus was buried in Seville, as was his son Diego. Their bodies were exhumed in 1542, taken to Santo Domingo, and buried in the cathedral there.

Perhaps the greatest of all the early explorers, a man of vision, imagination, and courage, Columbus generally gets both too much credit and too much blame for the colonization of the Americas and the fate of Native American peoples since 1492. He was a poor administrator and not a very humane one, although he was probably no more or no less harsh in his treatment of native peoples than any other in his position at that time. Yet it was his voyage that began the chain of events that would eventually destroy so much of the Native American way of life. He was not the first in the Americas and not even the first European. But he was a skilled **mariner** who sailed safely into a world he did not even know existed.

He may not have been the first, but Columbus excited the imagination of other adventurers. He brought great excitement and renewed energy to Europe. Through the doors he opened came the thousands and thousands of Europeans who would change the history of North and South America.

A gold lantern burns continuously over the tomb of Christopher Columbus in Santo Domingo.

Chapter Two
The Brothers Pinzon
They Sailed with Columbus (1492)

Brothers Vincente Yanez and Martin Alonso Pinzon sailed on the historic voyage of Christopher Columbus in 1492. One would be remembered as a skilled navigator and successful explorer in his own right. The other would be remembered only for his disloyalty to his captain.

The brothers were born in Palos, Spain—Vincente in about 1460 and Martin about 20 years earlier. They came from a family of noted shipowners who took part in outfitting the first expedition of Columbus.

Commander of the Nina

Vicente Pinzon captained the *Nina,* the smallest of Columbus's three-ship fleet. Like the *Pinta* it was a **caravel,** about 50 or 60 tons (45 or 54 metric tons) and 49 feet (15 meters) long. But unlike most ships of that period, it had four masts instead of three, which made it the best of the three at sailing upwind. The *Nina* began the voyage with lateen sails, which

Martin Pinzon (c. 1440–1493) served as commander of the Pinta *on Columbus's first voyage.*

are triangular in shape and are very maneuverable when the wind changes a great deal. But in the Canary Islands, the *Nina* was outfitted with square sails like the others because Columbus rightly figured that the wind taking the ships west would be unchanging. The *Nina* carried about twenty crew members who generally slept on deck except in very bad weather.

An able and skilled sailor, Vicente Pinzon sailed with Columbus throughout his entire first voyage to the Americas. But early in 1500 he took his own expedition to the coast of Brazil, sailing from Palos with four caravels. During the four-month voyage, Vicente found the mouth of the Amazon River. He is believed to be the first European to have done so. From there he sailed north and reached the Gulf of Paria in Venezuela in early May. For his discoveries he was made governor of these lands but never took possession of them. Sailing northwest Vicente lost two ships near the Bahamas and returned to Palos in September.

In 1508 Vicente was commissioned to find a passage to the Spice Islands (present-day Moluccas in Indonesia), and he sailed along the coast of Central America with Juan Diaz de Solis. They may have been the first Europeans to see the coastline of Mexico. Details are vague about whether Vicente also saw Honduras and the Yucatan on this voyage, but he returned to Spain in 1509. Little is known of Vicente Pinzon after that. He died in Palos around 1523.

Commander of the *Pinta*

Martin Alonso Pinzon, older brother to Vicente, commanded the second largest of the three ships on the first voyage of Columbus. The *Pinta* was a 70-ton (64-metric-ton) caravel, about 56 feet (17 meters) long. It probably had three masts like the *Santa Maria*.

Martin was a skilled **mariner,** and it was his suggestion for a course change on October 7 that brought Columbus's expedition to landfall in the Bahamas on October 12. However, when the three ships were off the coast of Cuba on November 22, Martin suddenly left the fleet without the permission of his commander. After searching for gold, Martin rejoined the fleet. On the return trip to Spain he left the fleet once again. His ship was the fastest, and he hoped to be the first to reach Europe with the momentous news of the discovery.

But it was Christopher Columbus who arrived first to report about the wondrous journey. And Martin Pinzon is remembered, not for his explorations and skill as a mariner, but for his disloyalty to his commander. He died the following year, in 1493.

Chapter Three
Vasco Nuñez de Balboa
To the Pacific Shores (1511–1513)

He was only one of the many adventurers who followed the path set by Columbus in the 1400s. On a quest to discover and claim new lands for the Spanish empire, Vasco Nuñez de Balboa (1475–1519) became famous in two ways: He was the first European to establish a permanent settlement on the mainland of South America (1511) and, without official authority, he became the first to sight the Pacific Ocean from the western shore of the New World (1513).

First, the land

Balboa was born into a family of what was called "impoverished gentry." That meant they had a title but no money. His birthplace was Jerez de los Caballeros in the Spanish province of Estremadura. He is believed to have been one of four sons born to Don Nuno Arias de Balboa. There are few other details of his early years except that he served as a page for some time to nobleman Don Pedro Puertocarrero, Lord of Moguer. The House of Moguer had a maritime tradition and a special interest in the Indies. Some of its men had sailed with Columbus.

Those from families that were titled but had no wealth had to find some way to make a living above that of a common worker. It was not unusual at the time

A portrait shows Vasco Nuñez de Balboa (1475–1519) dressed in armor.

for such young men to go to the sea, especially on the many expeditions sailing to the Americas. So in 1501 Balboa joined the voyage of Rodrigo de Bastidas, a wealthy retired **mariner,** and Juan de la Cosa, an experienced mapmaker and explorer, to Hispaniola (an island now shared by Haiti and the

Dominican Republic). After hearing reports of Columbus's voyages, Bastidas was inspired to look for pearls on the northern coast of South America.

Bastidas was successful and was able to trade European goods for pearls and gold, as was Balboa. The expedition crossed the Gulf of Uraba (on the coast of modern-day Colombia), where Balboa first saw what is now Panama and a Native American village he called Darien. According to some reports, their ship began to leak and they had to land and abandon ship at Hispaniola.

Balboa went to Santo Domingo and tried to make a living as a planter and farmer. He was so poor at the job that he was soon in great debt and hounded by creditors. Desperate to get away, in 1510 he hid himself and his dog Leoncico in a huge barrel on a ship in the harbor at Santo Domingo. The vessel, one of two commanded by Martin Fernandez de Enciso, was taking supplies to the Spanish colony of San Sebastian on the Gulf of Uraba. The colony had been founded by Alonso de Ojeda.

The first settlement

On the way to San Sebastian, Balboa and his dog were discovered and soon accepted as members of the crew. In fact Enciso, who was a poor leader, seemed glad to have Balboa at his side. When the ship stopped at Cartagena (Colombia), a brigantine commanded by Francisco Pizarro, whom Ojeda had left in command at San Sebastian, was in the harbor. Pizarro reported that his entire colony had been wiped out by disease and Native American attacks. Enciso decided to sail to San Sebastian anyway and persuaded Pizarro to follow him. But Enciso's ship was wrecked entering the harbor at San Sebastian and lost all its supplies and livestock.

The colony was indeed in ruins. Balboa remembered the Native American village of Darien he had seen on the voyage with Bastidas. He suggested that site was a more suitable location for a colony. It was agreed and they proceeded to Darien where the Spaniards subdued or drove out the native peoples, took over, and set up a headquarters. The town of Santa Maria de la Antigua del Darien was founded.

Balboa now cleverly arranged to make himself the undisputed leader of the colony. First, he convinced the colonists that Enciso had no authority in the new settlement. That was not difficult because Enciso was as inept on land as at sea. He soon returned to Spain. Then, Diego de Nicuesa arrived as the king's new governor. Balboa persuaded the colonists to reject him, which they did. Next, the colonists chose Balboa and a man named

Zamudio to rule as joint mayors. But Balboa got him out of the way by giving him gold to take back to Spain. Balboa was now the undisputed leader of the first stable settlement on the mainland of South America. In 1511 he learned that the king had named him temporary governor of the colony until the matter could be settled.

Balboa may have been brash, but he was no fool. If he were to make a name for himself and acquire any wealth, he had better plan wisely and get started before Spanish authorities interfered.

For two years Balboa demonstrated a gift for making friends and trading with the local native peoples surrounding his colony. Those who proved unfriendly were captured, tortured, and killed, and their villages were looted. One way or another, Balboa became a very rich man. He also proved skilled at dividing one native group against another by forming alliances. The Native Americans around Darien were generally less warlike than others. They usually fled at the sight of the Spanish and their attack dogs, which terrified the native peoples by sometimes tearing their victims to pieces.

On their expedition to the Pacific, Balboa and his men had to cross through difficult terrain in the jungles of what is now Panama.

To the sea

Balboa also sent many gold- and slave-hunting expeditions into the main Native American strongholds in the region. Many times in his dealings with friendly native peoples he heard stories of a great sea beyond the mountains and of a gold-rich land called Biru (Peru). These were surely references to the Pacific Ocean and the Inca Empire to the south. Balboa was told that he would need at least 1,000 men to capture this land. He became convinced the stories were true. He sent a message to the king requesting 1,000 men for a voyage of great discovery.

King Ferdinand was impressed, and a large expedition was organized immediately. The group of 2,000 left Spain in April 1514. There was just one problem as far as Balboa was concerned. He was not going to lead the expedition. Command was given to the elderly but powerful nobleman Pedro Arias Davila, usually known as Pedriarias.

However, well before Pedriarias left Spain, Balboa had received news that he was in trouble at the royal court. He heard that the king was sending an order for him to return to Spain and explain his treatment of both Enciso and Nicuesa at Darien.

Balboa quickly mounted an unofficial expedition of his own. On September 1, 1513, he sailed from Darien with about 190 Spaniards, 800 Native Americans, and several dogs, including Leoncico. He dropped anchor at Acla, which luckily turned out to be the narrowest site in the **isthmus** of Panama. He left the vessels in the care of about half his crew and started the journey south across the isthmus.

For the next several days, Balboa and his men cut their way through some of the most impenetrable terrain in the world. There are still no roads in many parts of that area. It is a land of dense jungle, swamps, rivers, crocodiles, snakes, and endless insects. The heat was unbearable, especially to the Spanish who wore heavy armor and carried burdensome weapons. It took about 4 days to go 30 miles. There was also the added threat of Native American attack. It is said that in one particularly fierce fight, the Spanish killed about 600 Native Americans. From these battles and from looting Native American villages, the Spaniards became quite wealthy on this journey.

Balboa could never had made it across the isthmus without the help of guides. He devised a method of obtaining them that was used by all the conquistadors who followed him. When the Native Americans fled from a village as the Spaniards approached, Balboa persuaded them to return by offering gifts to the chief. In return, he would ask for some village members to act as guides. They were often given gold as well. When he reached another village, he would send the guides back and take on new ones.

In this way, and after extreme hardships, near the end of September Balboa climbed a hill and became the first European to see the Pacific Ocean from its eastern shore. According to legend the sighting occurred on Sunday, September 25, 1513. Balboa was alone except for his faithful dog. That may be just a story because other reports say the first sighting was on September 27, a Tuesday. Had it really occurred on a Sunday, that fact would likely have been emphasized in the journals.

Whatever the day, Vasco Nuñez de Balboa had made his mark in history. Shortly afterward the rest of the party, including Pizarro, joined him. They erected a pile of stones and a cross and sang a Catholic hymn of thanksgiving,

33

Balboa and his men see the Pacific from a hill in present-day Panama.

"Te Deum." The entire party then marched down to the shore, which took a few days. Supposedly Balboa, in full armor and sheathed sword, waded into the surf and lifted the Spanish banner. He took possession of the ocean, islands, and all surrounding land for Spain. He named the site Bahia San Miguel (St. Michael's Bay). Balboa called the ocean "the Southern Sea" because at the point where he first saw it, he was facing south. It would be another seven years before Ferdinand Magellan called it the Pacific.

The last adventure

Balboa and his men spent about a month on the Pacific shore. They visited the Pearl Islands and collected gold and pearls. They returned by a different route and ran into Native American attacks once again but lost no men in the battles. The return trip proved almost as hazardous as before. This was largely because the Spaniards were so loaded down with **loot** that they could carry very little food. Many of them nearly died of starvation. Balboa himself came down with a fever and had to be carried into the settlement at Darien, which they reached on January 19, 1514. They had been gone more than four months.

Balboa returned to find Pedrarias, the new head of government, waiting for him. Pedrarias was an ill-natured man with poor governing skills who almost instantly took a dislike to the younger and popular Balboa. Supposedly Pedrarias questioned Balboa about giving a soldier's share of the captured loot to his dog, Leoncico. Balboa said that was true but the men had agreed to it because Leoncico was as good as any soldier.

Word of Balboa's discovery of the "Southern Sea" brought him back to favor in the royal court. He was given the title of adelantado (admiral), just as Columbus had been, for the provinces of Panama and Coiba (Cuba). However, he was still subject to the authority of Pedrarias.

Such an arrangement was never going to work. Friction between the two men deepened. Pedrarias would not give Balboa permission to embark on any further expeditions. Finally, in 1515 Pedrarias relented and gave Balboa grudging permission to explore along the coast of the Pacific.

Over the next three years, Balboa mounted a truly amazing expedition. He decided to build the ships right on the ocean shore. This meant cutting huge amounts of timber and dragging them and all necessary supplies through the treacherous route of mountains and jungle. Records of the undertaking praise Balboa and the Spaniards for completing such a difficult task, but it was actually the Native American slaves who did the work, and hundreds of them died in the process.

Initially Balboa planned to build four vessels. However, after transporting all the wood it was discovered that much of

An engraving shows Balboa taking possession of the Pacific.

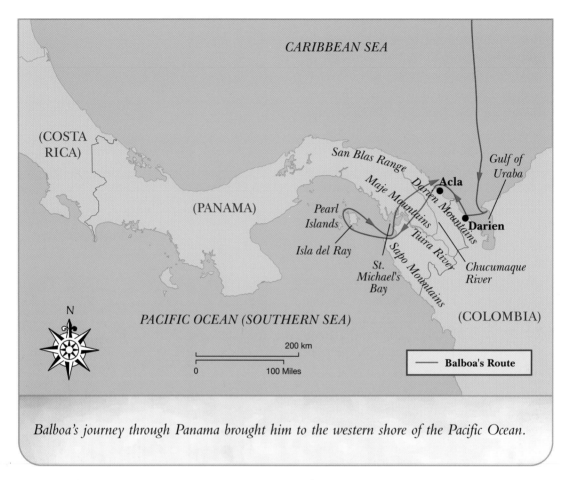

Balboa's journey through Panama brought him to the western shore of the Pacific Ocean.

it was useless because it was infested with fungus. He finally set out to sea in two ships, which were nearly destroyed by bad weather. Balboa returned to shore and planned to build two more ships before setting out again. He noted in his journal that it might be a good idea to cut a channel through the **isthmus** for easy passage. This idea was realized about 400 years later with the construction of the Panama Canal.

Treason!

Back in Darien Pedrarias had learned that the crown was planning to send a new governor to replace him and that he would be subject to a review of his conduct in office. Doubtless fearing that Balboa would testify against him, Pedrarias summoned the explorer back to Darien. To make sure that Balboa answered the summons, Pedrarias sent a force to the Pacific coast to get him, but Balboa offered no resistance.

Once in Darien Balboa was charged with treason. Pedrarias accused him of plotting to abandon the Spanish king and set up in his own colony in Peru. Balboa was also accused of mistreatment of the native peoples, rebellion, and other misdeeds. The townspeople, with whom Balboa was highly popular, protested. However a sham trial presided over by Gaspar de Espinosa, Pedrarias's own chief justice, found him guilty. Balboa was beheaded in the public square sometime between January 13 and 21, 1519. Pedrarias, who died in 1531, was later held responsible for the explorer's trial and death.

Whatever his faults, Vasco Nuñez de Balboa was never a traitor to his king or his country. There is no record of his plotting to set up a colony in Peru. Instead, another Spanish explorer, Francisco Pizarro, would later venture to Peru and destroy the prosperous civilization of the Incas.

Spain lost one of its bravest captains with Balboa's death. Brash and even cruel, he was still an innovative explorer. His journey to the Pacific shore still stands as one of history's amazing adventures.

Today the Panama Canal connects the Atlantic and Pacific Oceans.

Chapter Four
Diego Velazquez de Cuellar
Taking Cuba (1511–1521)

Hailed as the Spanish conquistador who founded the island of Cuba and ruled as its governor for more than a decade, Diego Velazquez de Cuellar (1465–1524) destroyed a native people in the process. He is also indirectly responsible for the destruction of Aztec Mexico and the Mayan Yucatan.

To the New World

So little is known about the early years of Velazquez that even his birthplace is in doubt. Most historians believe he was born in Cuellar near Segovia, Spain, in about 1465. However, there are no records of his baptism there between 1450 and 1480, so perhaps he was born in a nearby village. He is believed to have fought in Spain's war with Italy as a young man.

In 1493 Velazquez sailed to the New World on the second voyage of Christopher Columbus. He settled in Hispaniola, the island now occupied by Haiti and the Dominican Republic, and became a prominent landowner. Handsome and confident, he was an able administrator and colonizer. Even Bartolome de Las Casas approved of him. Las Casas was the Dominican missionary in the Americas who first exposed the oppression of native people by the Europeans.

A portrait of Diego Velazquez de Cuellar (1465–1524)

By 1501 Columbus was no longer the governing authority over Spanish claims in the Americas, but Velazquez now held a high office on Hispaniola. In 1511 Columbus's son Diego sent Velazquez to the island of Cuba as its adelantado, or governor. The Spanish king was anxious to learn if Cuba would produce any gold. Velazquez was chosen because of his reputation as a courageous and fierce fighter, and no one knew what resistance the Spaniards might face.

Governor of Cuba

With three or four ships and about 300 men, Velazquez sailed for Cuba, accompanied by his trusted aide, Panfilo de Narvaez, and Las Casas, who served as chaplain of the expedition even though he was not yet a priest. Some two years earlier, it had been learned that Cuba was indeed an island and not part of the Asian mainland as Columbus had first thought. The conquest would have been easy and perhaps bloodless because the native peoples of Cuba were not warlike. But Velazquez did not want only to subdue them, he wanted to break their will to resist.

Velazquez landed on the eastern end of Cuba at Maisi. He preceded a smaller force coming from Jamaica and led by Narvaez, which landed on Cuba's southern coast near the Gulf of Guacanayabo. When they met, the two forces divided their men into three groups, one going inland, one along the northern coast, and one sailing the southern shores. They set Carenas (now Havana) Bay as their meeting point.

Although the Native Americans were far more bewildered than dangerous, the Spaniards carried out a **massacre** on the island. As many as 2,000 Native Americans were reported slaughtered in the village of Caonao. It was at this point that Las Casas began to have doubts about Spanish designs on the island. He reported that not one Spanish soldier died in the fighting.

Shortly after the conquest of Cuba, Las Casas became a priest. Although he had been a participant in the destruction of

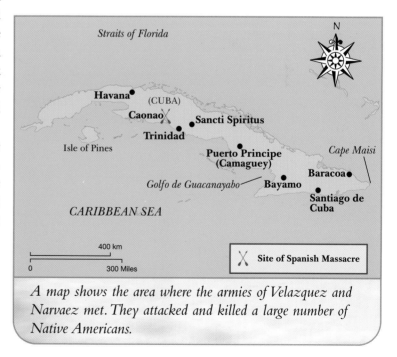

A map shows the area where the armies of Velazquez and Narvaez met. They attacked and killed a large number of Native Americans.

With a population of over two million people, Havana is the largest city in the Caribbean region.

the native people, he now devoted his life to better treatment of Native Americans.

With all Native American resistance gone, over the next four years until about 1514 Velazquez and his men founded the settlements of Baracoa, Bayamo, Santiago, Puerto Principe, Sancti Spiritus, and Havana. Some areas were found to contain gold. Velazquez established his capital at Baracoa where he eventually built a fortress. It was the first settlement in Cuba to be called a city, and it received a coat of arms. Today's Cuban capital of Havana first

began as a settlement on the Gulf of Batabano, but was later moved to its current location on the northern coast.

Except for his brutal treatment of Native Americans, Velazquez was generally considered to be a good leader and administrator. He began to encourage colonists to settle in Cuba. When Cristobal de Cuellar, treasurer of the Indies, arrived with his daughter, Dona Maria, Velazquez asked for her hand in marriage. Unfortunately the young bride died in less than a week from unknown causes.

With gold discovered in the island hills, many fortune seekers were anxious to go to Cuba. Velazquez first took land from the native people to give to his friends, including Hernan Cortes, and then took the Native Americans themselves to be given away. Despite the new Spanish laws that laid down restrictions for what amounted to slavery, Velazquez put virtually no restrictions on himself concerning the lives of the native people of Cuba. When the new laws specified that it was illegal to round up Native Americans to be given away in groups, Velazquez got around that by specifying that the Native Americans were not permanent slaves since they would be held for only specified periods of time. About the only word from the king that could be called a restriction was the edict that Velazquez should teach the Native Americans Catholicism and treat them so as to "best preserve their lives."

During the eight-year administration of Velazquez, Cuba's Native American population dropped from about 112,000 to about 3,000. As horrendous as those figures sound today, they would not have raised an eyebrow in most of the other European colonies in the New World. If the Native Americans did not die at the hands of the newcomers, they died from

Wild pigs, like the one shown in this painting, were brought to Cuba from Europe. They caused a great deal of destruction to the Cuban farmland.

diseases unwittingly brought from Europe on the sailing vessels. They also died from the thousands of wild pigs that the Spaniards brought with them. The pigs had no enemies on the island and ran wild, destroying cultivated land and leaving the native peoples without food. Thousands died from starvation. Untold numbers committed suicide, often killing their children first rather than have them face the torture of the conquerors.

Exploring Mexico

In 1515 Velazquez moved his capital to Santiago de Cuba on the southeastern coast. That made for easier sailing lanes with Hispaniola and Jamaica. Shipping was increasing rapidly with the flow of gold leaving the island. Gold, and his reputation for good administration, made Velazquez a person of renown in the New World. When he heard reports of a mainland to the west, Velazquez sought more glory. He sent expeditions to the Yucatan **Peninsula** and to the Gulf of Mexico by Francisco de Cordoba in 1517 and by Juan de Grijalva in 1518. Reports described a land of great wealth and beauty, and carried rumors of a wondrous empire.

Grijalva landed on the island of Cozumel at the eastern end of Yucatan and then sailed to about 50 miles (80 kilometers) from present-day Veracruz. He met **emissaries** of Montezuma, the Aztec ruler of Mexico. He also sent a messenger and some gold back to Cuba.

Velazquez would come to regret these expeditions to the mainland. As the crown became more interested in the land that would be called South America, its interest in Cuba and the other islands in the Caribbean decreased. Deciding that Grijalva needed assistance and perhaps to enhance his own dwindling importance, Velazquez sent Hernan Cortes to the mainland of Mexico in 1518. But now his troubles really began.

With an **armada** of about 300 men and 6 ships, Cortes sailed to Mexico and founded Veracruz on the Mexican Gulf. Then Cortes followed the example of his own leader and set himself up as sole leader on the mainland, ignoring the authority of Velazquez. In fact once Cortes made contact with the Aztec empire, he destroyed most of his own ships so that there would be no chance to return to Cuba.

The suspicion that Cortes was going to establish himself as governor of what seemed to be a vast empire in Mexico was more than Velazquez could tolerate. He knew it could be the richest and biggest Spanish colony of all. First, Velazquez appealed to the crown, arguing that Cortes was overstepping his authority. But when Cortes began sending back enormous amounts of gold from his new discovery, the crown was not so inclined to discipline him.

Finally, in 1519, with **smallpox** and measles devastating the Cuban colony, Velazquez sent an expedition after Cortes. It was led by Narvaez, who was given 13 ships and more than 1,000 men to bring Cortes back to Cuba. Cortes, who was in the Aztec capital of Tenochtitlan at the time, heard of the mission and surprised Narvaez in Veracruz. Narvaez was captured and imprisoned. To add to the bitterness of the defeat, Cortes persuaded all the soldiers under Narvaez to join his side.

A losing cause

Once again Velazquez complained to the crown, now held by Charles V, who would become Holy Roman Emperor in 1519. Velazquez was given an order of arrest for Cortes. But after Cortes destroyed the ancient Aztec city and great riches poured into the Spanish court, a new order came

This cathedral stands in present-day Santiago de Cuba.

from Spain. It told Velazquez to keep his hands off Mexico.

It was a bitter defeat and disgrace for the conquistador. He lost money by financing the last expedition and he lost prestige when Cortes overstepped his authority. It was especially disgraceful that Cortes had been able to persuade Velazquez's own soldiers to join him.

Early in 1521 Alonso Zuazo arrived in Cuba to replace Velazquez as governor. But the lure of riches apparently mesmerized Zuazo as well and he proved to be a poor leader. Velazquez, living in Santiago de Cuba, once more complained, and King Charles removed Zuazo from his post.

The administration of Cuba continued to decline and with it Velazquez's hopes for a great empire on the island. To pursue his now ruined dreams of glory, he had destroyed a native people. Diego Velazquez de Cuellar died of a stroke in Cuba in June 1524.

Chapter Five
Francisco de Cordoba and Juan de Grijalva
The Door to Mexico (1517, 1518)

A portrait depicts Juan de Grijalva (c.1489–1524).

Explorers Francisco de Cordoba and Juan de Grijalva are little more than footnotes in the story of Spanish conquests in the Americas. Yet they opened the door to Mexico for Spain and for Hernan Cortes, who followed them.

Cordoba

Francisco de Cordoba (c.1489–1524) was the first European to explore the Yucatan **peninsula** in eastern Mexico and the first to come in contact with the ancient Mayan civilization. He was sent to Mexico by Diego Velazquez, governor of Cuba, in February 1517 with three ships and 110 soldiers. His mission was to look for riches and to explore the region.

Cordoba landed on what he thought was an island and called it Yucatan. He found a civilization with a long, cultured history of its own, the Mayans. They date their ancestry back to greatness in about the year 250 C.E. At their height the Mayans had more than 40 cities, each with a population of about 5,000 to 50,000. Mayan cities contained pyramids, palaces, and plazas. Their agriculture was based on cultivation of corn, beans, and squash. They had developed a calendar and a system of **hieroglyphic** writing. They made paper from fig trees and wrote books, known as codices. Their sculpture and relief carving were extraordinary. The causes of the Mayan decline are uncertain, but by the time of Cordoba's arrival, the Mayan people were basically village dwellers and farmers.

Cordoba sent back reports about this civilization he had uncovered, including the fact that the Mayans practiced human sacrifice. He also offered some evidence that there was gold and silver in the region. However, the Mayans were hostile to the Spanish invasion, and nearly half of Cordoba's men died in battle.

Cordoba later explored Nicaragua and founded the first permanent Spanish settlements in the area, including Granada on Lake Nicaragua and León near Lake Managua. He died in 1524.

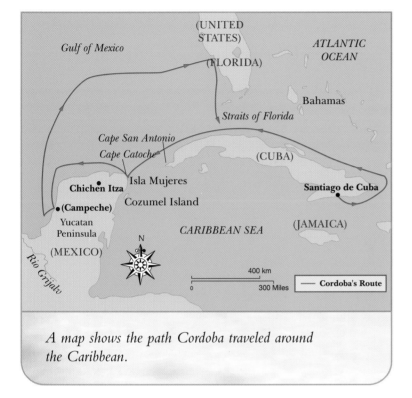

A map shows the path Cordoba traveled around the Caribbean.

Grijalva

A nephew of Diego Velazquez, Juan de Grijalva (1480–1527) was also from Cuellar in Spain. He had sailed to Cuba with his uncle and went to Santo Domingo in 1508. On May 1, 1518, Velazquez named him captain-general and sent him on another expedition to Mexico. Grijalva sailed from San Anton and three days later landed on an island he called Cozumel on the eastern side of the Yucatan peninsula.

After many battles with native peoples, Grijalva was finally welcomed at a village near the modern city of Veracruz. He formally took possession of the region for the Spanish crown. When Grijalva began to explore inland, he came upon two stone temples with steps leading up to altars. There was also evidence of human sacrifice.

Grijalva has been criticized for not founding a settlement in the region he had explored. Some experts cite the fact that after four months of exploration and battle with native peoples, he had few men and fewer supplies to attempt a settlement. Instead Grijalva sent his largest ship back to Cuba with the gold ornaments he had obtained. Perhaps he hoped that the sight of gold would convince Velazquez to send reinforcements. But bad weather and lack of supplies finally persuaded Grijalva to return to Cuba himself.

Although Grijalva had helped to open the door to Mexico for the Spanish, his uncle regarded his expedition as a failure. Velazquez needed more than evidence of gold. He wanted to give the king a new empire in the New World. Grijalva had failed. Now the door was open for Hernan Cortes.

Chapter Six
Hernan Cortes
Destroyer of the Aztecs, Conqueror of Mexico (1519–1521

H ernan Cortes (1485–1547) is probably the most famous of all the Spanish conquerors in the Americas. He was an explorer of truly remarkable achievements. Cortes won Mexico for the Spanish crown. He conquered the mighty Aztecs and their empire that was four times the size of his own country. He seized an astounding amount of wealth in gems, silver, and gold. He increased the population of the Spanish empire by about 25 million people. And he did it all with only a few thousand soldiers.

In achieving all these amazing feats, the 16th-century explorer destroyed an entire civilization and the Aztec capital city of Tenochtitlan. He and his men pulled down cities and rebuilt them in the European style. Thousands of Native Mexicans were killed by Cortes and his soldiers. Perhaps as many as 18 million out of a total population of 25 million died of diseases brought from overseas. First called a fair-skinned god and later a brutal tyrant, Hernan Cortes changed Central America and his native Spain forever.

Restless in Estremadura

To be born a male in Estremadura in the 1500s was to be born to fight. This province in southwestern Spain was

A portrait of Hernan Cortes (1485–1547)

home to adventurers and soldiers of fortune. These were men who had conquered the land for their king and for the Catholic faith. Hernan Cortes was born in Estremadura in 1485 into a family of minor nobility. His father, Martin Cortes de Monroy, had served honorably in the Spanish infantry. However, neither he nor his wife, Dona

Catalina Pizarro Altamarino, wanted their son to become a soldier. At an early age they recognized Hernan's intelligence and cleverness. They also recognized that he was arrogant, quarrelsome, and a bit of a headache to raise. So when he was fourteen, they sent him to Salamanca in west central Spain to study law.

Hernan lasted only two years in Salamanca, returning home in 1501 without a law degree, much to his parents' dismay. However, he had gained a good understanding of Spanish law, which would be of help to him in later years. He also became quite an accomplished writer while in law school. But Cortes had returned home because he was frustrated by the quiet life in Spain. His imagination had been fired by the stories of Christopher Columbus and his great discoveries in an unknown world.

Cortes had the chance to sail with Nicolas de Ovando, who was going to the Spanish Indies in 1501. However, he was injured so badly in a fall from a wall that he was unable to sail. He spent the next year idling around the coastal port of Valencia. In 1504 his family raised enough money to send him to the island of Hispaniola (now Santo Domingo), which Columbus had visited just twelve years earlier. Cortes was nineteen years old.

In Hispaniola and Cuba

For the next seven years, Cortes was a farmer and notary in the town of Azua, about 50 miles (80 kilometers) west of Santo Domingo. Because he was sick with an infectious disease, he missed the ill-fated expeditions of Diego de Nicuesa and Alonso de Ojeda to the South American mainland in 1509.

Two years later Cortes had recovered enough to accompany Diego Velazquez on his mission to conquer the island of Cuba. When Velazquez was appointed governor, Cortes was named clerk to the treasurer, which meant he received land, slaves, and the first house built in the new capital of Santiago in the eastern part of the island. With this new status he assumed a position of some power in the colony and was often at odds with his superior, Velazquez. Friction between them increased when Cortes started a romance with Catalina Juarez, the sister of Velazquez's mistress. According to the story, Cortes had promised to marry Catalina but then changed his mind, which infuriated Velazquez. When Cortes did marry Catalina, he renewed his friendship with Velazquez.

Twice appointed mayor, or alcalde, of Santiago, Cortes became a rich man by mining gold and raising livestock. In his dress, conversation, and bearing, he began to act much like a great lord.

Cortes's fleet sails out of the harbor of Santiago, Cuba.

In 1517 Velazquez sent Francisco Hernandez de Cordoba to the Yucatan **Peninsula** on the mainland. Although the expedition suffered heavy casualties from a meeting with armed Mayan warriors, Cordoba brought back reports of a highly civilized people. The following April Velazquez sent a larger expedition headed by his nephew, Juan de Grijalva, to investigate Cordoba's reports and establish a colony on the mainland.

When Velazquez decided that Grijalva needed assistance, he named Cortes as captain general of a new expedition in October 1518. At his headquarters in Santiago, Cortes assembled a force of about six ships and 300 men in less than a month. He did this with his great ability as a speaker and his long experience as an administrator. Cortes also had a flair for the dramatic. In his recruiting, he marched around the city with his followers carrying a banner that said, "Brothers and Comrades, let us follow the sign of the Holy Cross in true faith, for under this sign we shall conquer." Even though, like all the conquistadors and explorers of the period, personal wealth was always a consideration, these men also had a very real sense that they were doing something of great importance for the Catholic Church. To be Spanish in the 1500s meant to be Catholic.

All this dramatic recruiting only inflamed Velazquez's jealousy toward his subordinate and he began to fear Cortes's popularity. He also began to have second thoughts about who should head the expedition. Wisely figuring that Velazquez might change his mind, Cortes hastily sailed from Santiago on November 18, 1518. When Velazquez heard of the departure, he was furious but helpless.

Cortes stopped at Trinidad to add to his **armada.** When he sailed for the Yucatan in February, he had amassed a force of 11 ships, 508 soldiers, 100 sailors, 14 cannons, and—very importantly—16 horses. He also had the undying animosity of Velazquez.

The expedition to Mexico

When Cortes landed on the coast of Yucatan, he did what no other explorer or conquistador had done before him. He disciplined and exercised his army until it was molded into a cohesive force. And then he burned most of his ships. With that act he had committed himself and his men to survival by conquest. They would all succeed on the mainland or they would all die on the mainland.

Like Grijalva before him, Cortes landed at Cozumel where he located a castaway from a wrecked Spanish ship. Jeronimo de Aguilar had been stranded on the mainland for eight years and agreed to act as interpreter. The next stop was Tabasco on the coast near the mouth of the Grijalva River. The native peoples wanted nothing to do with the newcomers and rejected their demands for supplies. Cortes attacked the town and captured it. A few days later, a large

Cortes and his men unload their cargo on the coast of Mexico.

force of Native Americans tried to push the Europeans into the sea but were defeated by Spanish heavy artillery.

Cortes now decided to find and defeat the Aztec empire if it existed. At least part of his astounding success can be attributed to his good luck at this point. He forced the defeated native people of Tabasco to turn over a number of slaves. One of them was a young woman named Malinche, given the title of Dona Marina by the Spaniards.

Also part of Cortes's success story was his great ability to assess a situation quickly. He immediately saw what a help she could be to him. This amazing woman was a captured princess who spoke Nahuatl, the language of the Aztecs. Not only did Dona Marina become his interpreter but also his adviser on all things relating to the native people of Mexico. Eventually she became his mistress and sometimes his spy. Later they would have a son, Martin. He was one of the first so-called mestizos, a person of mixed Native American and Spanish ancestry.

Cortes sailed farther west, where he founded the town of Veracruz. Using his knowledge of Spanish law, he cleverly had his men elect him captain and chief justice of the settlement. This meant that his power now rested on the civic rights of a town under the Spanish

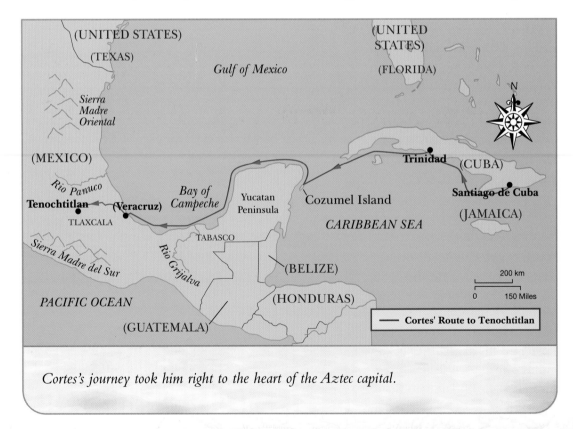

Cortes's journey took him right to the heart of the Aztec capital.

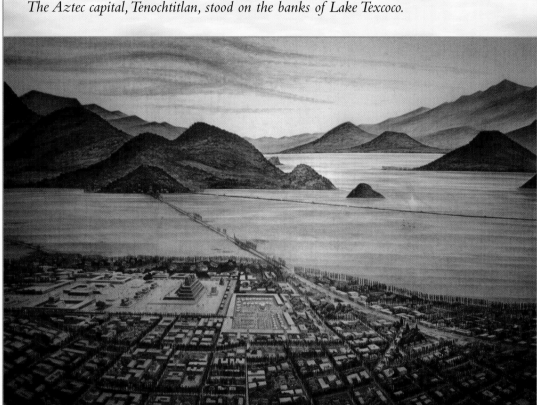

The Aztec capital, Tenochtitlan, stood on the banks of Lake Texcoco.

crown, not on his appointment by Velazquez. At Veracruz, Cortes received his first messenger from the Aztec king Montezuma and first learned the legend of the Aztec god Quetzalcoatl, who was expected at some time to return from across the sea.

The Aztec world

The people that Cortes was about to confront in Mexico in 1519 were part of a proud civilization of confident warriors at the height of their glory. In less than three years, what had taken them centuries to build was destroyed forever.

The Aztecs were probably people of the northern Mexican plateau who migrated to islands in Lake Texcoco around the year 1325 and founded their capital city, Tenochtitlan. The name means "place of the prickly pear cactus." At its height, the city covered about 5 square miles (13 square kilometers) and was home to about 140,000 inhabitants. By 1519 the total population of the Aztec empire was perhaps as much as six million people

Aztec priests perform human sacrifice at the great temple of Tenochtitlan.

Le grand Temple de Mexique.

spread over about 80,000 square miles (207,200 square kilometers).

The basis of Aztec success in establishing a great state and empire was their remarkable system of agriculture. All available land was cultivated, and flourished under an elaborate network of irrigation and reclamation of swampland. The result was a rich and populous state. It was also a disciplined one. The Aztecs had no prisons, nor did they need any. Anyone convicted of a crime was dealt with quickly. A convicted murderer had his head crushed with a heavy stone. Someone who lied about her neighbor had her lips cut off. Thieves were tied to posts in the marketplace and stoned until they died. Anyone who got drunk in public was put to death on the spot, unless he or she were elderly. Aztecs believed the elderly should be left alone because they would soon be traveling to a spirit world.

The military played a dominant role in Aztec life, with valor in war being the quickest way to success. Priests and **bureaucrats** ran the society, with different classes of serfs, **indentured servants,** and slaves at the bottom. Religion was also a great and controlling force. The Aztecs believed that earth was the latest in a series of creations. Their main gods were Huitzilopochtli, god of war; Tonatiuh, god of the sun; Tlaloc, god of rain; and Quetzalcoatl, the Feathered Serpent, part god and part folk hero. The Aztecs regularly practiced human sacrifices to the sun god. If the sun god did not receive a steady diet of human blood, the Aztecs believed the world would die. It was a common sight to see victims, usually captured in wars, marching in a single-file line up the 114 steps of the Great Pyramid at Tenochtitlan to have their hearts torn out and, while still beating, held toward the sun.

It was partly this practice of human sacrifice, plus its strong, often brutal hold over subjected peoples, that were beginning to weaken the far-flung Aztec empire when Cortes arrived. Needless to say, other civilizations in Mexico would have been glad to see the Aztecs and their sacrificial practices destroyed forever.

The leader of the Aztecs and ninth Aztec emperor of Mexico was Montezuma II (1466–1520). His name means "angry young lord." When he succeeded his uncle Ahuitzotl in 1502,

his empire stretched into what is now Honduras and Nicaragua. However, it was showing signs of weakness as many native groups resented the increasing demands for tribute and victims for religious sacrifices. Montezuma was commander of the Aztec army and a figure of much discipline and learning, but he was also greatly influenced by his belief in the god of war. As part of his religious beliefs, Montezuma feared the return of the white-bearded god, Quetzalcoatl, who would one day come to take over the rule of the empire. Instead Montezuma met Cortes, a fair-skinned, white-bearded Spanish man who would not only take over the empire but would also destroy it.

The grand plan

On Easter Sunday 1519, thousands of Aztecs, led by a local governor named Tentlil, presented themselves to Cortes in Veracruz. They came bearing gifts including gold, silver, **incense,** and food offerings. Tentlil, as the ambassador for Montezuma, was very gracious to the Spanish. Cortes began to suspect that the Aztec king might be fearful that he, Cortes, was actually the dreaded Quetzalcoatl, come to regain his kingdom. When Cortes asked when he might have a meeting with Montezuma, he was told that no meeting was possible. In fact he learned that the Aztecs had no intention of letting him enter their capital city. Ever since the Spaniards had been appearing along

The Sierra Madres are the principle mountain range of Mexico.

the Mexican coast, the Aztecs were afraid that this might signal the return of Quetzalcoatl.

Realizing that there must be a great storehouse of riches in the Aztec capital, Cortes was now more determined than ever to find it and make Mexico his own colony. He sent Aztec messengers back to the chief with some Spanish gifts and inquired about the possibility of trade between the two peoples. While he waited for Montezuma's reply, Native Americans from the city of Cempoala arrived in Veracruz. They told Cortes of their enslavement by the Aztecs. It was then that Cortes realized his grand plan for conquering the Aztec empire. By dividing the native peoples of Mexico and turning them against each other, he would conquer them all. Cortes gave

gifts to the Cempoalans and assured them of his aid in freeing them from the harsh rule of the Aztecs.

Cortes then took two more steps to assure his authority in Mexico. He loaded one of his remaining ships with all the treasure he had so far collected from the Aztecs—a staggering amount of gold and silver—and sent it back to the king of Spain. Then he burned his last remaining ships. This was a final signal to all those who doubted him, Spanish and Native Americans alike: There was no way out but to follow Cortes.

The march to Tenochtitlan

On August 15, 1519, Cortes left Veracruz with his small army of about 300 soldiers and several hundred Native American warriors. He began his famous march through the mountains of Mexico to find Montezuma and the city of the Aztecs. The journey would take 83 days and cover 400 miles (644 kilometers). Taking the advice of the Cempoalans, Cortes planned his route through Tlaxcala, a mountainous region whose people hated the Aztecs and would, Cortes hoped, offer support to the Spanish party.

On the way, Cortes encountered a number of Aztec messengers, always polite but firm in their desire to have the Spaniards turn back. Cortes also met other native peoples who told them about their own encounters with the Aztecs. Slowly, Cortes began to realize

An engraving shows the first meeting between Montezuma II and Cortez in Mexico City.

what a rich and powerful empire he was determined to conquer.

By September the little army was high in the mountains. As they neared the land of the Tlaxcalans, Cortes sent messengers to speak of his peaceful intentions. A few days later, the reply came in the form of about 6,000 Tlaxcalans who attacked on September 5. Startled to find enemies where they had expected allies, the Spanish fought desperately but were in danger of losing the battle against such odds.

Cortes used cleverness to win the fight. First, he quickly had all 45 of his dead soldiers buried so that the Tlaxcalans would think their warriors had killed no one. Then he sent messengers to the Tlaxcalan camp to boldly warn the enemy that if they did not make peace, the Spanish would destroy their city.

It worked and a peace treaty was arranged. Tlaxcala joined the side of the Spanish, increasing the size of their army and its supplies. After a rest to recover from its wounds, the army marched toward Cholula, a major commercial center. Although the people there seemed to greet them as allies, Dona Marina soon uncovered a plot. Montezuma had ordered the Cholulans to trap the Spaniards within the city and kill them. For revenge Cortes planned a trick of his own. Explaining that he and his army would be leaving for the Aztec capital in the morning, Cortes asked the Cholulan chief to have thousands of his warriors and dignitaries in the city center for a farewell ceremony. The chief agreed. The following morning, the 3,000 or more Cholulans in the city square were surprised and quickly slaughtered by Spanish gunfire. Another Mexican stronghold had fallen to Cortes.

In early November 1519, Cortes climbed the snow-covered mountains to look upon the spectacular volcano of Popocatepetl and down into the valley at the sprawling city of Tenochtitlan. Leading an army of about 7,000 troops, Cortes entered the great metropolis of the Aztecs.

Whether Montezuma truly believed Cortes to be the god Quetzalocoatl or was merely sizing up an enemy, the Aztec chief was polite. He presented a splendid picture to the Spaniards as he stepped from his litter, his body clothed in a brilliant feathered robe covered with pearls, his head and feet sparkling with gold in the morning sun. Cortes dismounted and placed a string of inexpensive stones around the chief's neck. The Aztecs were shocked, for no one was allowed to touch their king. But Montezuma merely responded by putting two gold necklaces around the neck of Cortes. Then he invited Cortes to stay in a palace.

Cortes stayed in Tenochtitlan to survey the wealth of the city but made little progress in conquering the Aztecs. However, when word reached him that the Aztecs had killed two Spanish men in Veracruz, Cortes placed Montezuma under arrest. He was treated well and Montezuma accepted his imprisonment with good grace, apparently believing by this time that Cortes was indeed a god.

The downfall

In early May 1520, Cortes learned that Velazquez had sent Panfilo de Narvaez to Mexico to capture him. Technically, Velazquez cited disobedience by Cortes in taking over the Aztec city, but in reality Velazquez felt threatened by his rival's success and power. Cortes fled Tenochtitlan, leaving a small force behind with Pedro de Alvarado in charge. Cortes met Narvaez at the coast. He not only captured Narvaez but convinced most of the defeated army to join his forces.

The tired army returned to the Aztec city on June 24. What Cortes found spelled disaster. Alvarado had foolishly responded to an Aztec religious procession by attacking it. The furious Aztecs had driven the Spaniards back into a fortress and had burned bridges

Montezuma, a prisoner of the Spanish, is killed by an angry Aztec mob.

It was not until the night of June 30, 1520, known to the Spanish as Noche Triste or "sorrowful night," that Cortes and his men were able to sneak away from the city while the Aztec warriors were sleeping. They were attacked on the causeway and all but 400 of his soldiers were killed. Cortes had lost most of his army, including all of the Native American warriors who joined him. It is said that the great conquistador and conqueror of Mexico wept.

Conqueror of Mexico

After he and his remaining army recovered from their wounds in Tlaxcala, Cortes started the process of taking Tenochtitlan and conquering Mexico. Aided by reinforcements from Cuba, he marched back to the valley of Mexico in December. Cortes methodically captured the small towns around the capital city, effectively cutting off water and food supplies. In addition, during the Spanish occupation thousands of Aztecs had been infected with **smallpox,** from which most died. With his enemies weakened, Cortes was able to take Tenochtitlan. However, the Aztecs, now ruled by a new chief, Cuauhtemoc, refused to give up. Cortes took the city by destroying it, palace by palace, idol by idol, and stone by stone until, by the summer of 1521, nothing remained of the once great civilization of the Aztecs. Cuauhtemoc had no choice but to surrender on August 21, 1521.

to the city. Cortes realized that he and his men were trapped and might likely be destroyed.

Releasing Montezuma from prison, Cortes brought the Aztec leader to a rooftop, asking him to calm the people so that he and his men could leave the city. Instead the infuriated Aztecs shot stones from slings onto the rooftop. One of them struck Montezuma in the head. The leader of the Aztec empire died two days later, still a prisoner in his own city.

A little more than a year later, on October 22, 1522, King Charles V named Cortes governor and captain general of New Spain. At last, the long struggle for power between Cortes and Velazquez was over. Cortes started rebuilding the new city of Mexico on the ashes of the old Aztec center. He was now the ruler of a huge empire that extended from the Caribbean to the Pacific Ocean. Surprisingly, he was accepted by the native people as a fairly benign ruler. If the politics of the Spanish empire hadn't kept him in check, Cortes might indeed have become the independent ruler of his own empire in the New World.

A captive Cuauhtemoc is brought before Cortes.

The restless years

Even with such a vast empire to rule, Cortes was forever an explorer. He was an adventurer unable to resist the next unknown mountain or tale of fabulous wealth. He sent various expeditions around Mexico, one looking for a **strait** between the Atlantic and Pacific oceans. He sent Alvarado to Guatemala, where he conquered the land and the Mayans living there. He sent one of his most trusted soldiers, Cristobal de Olid, to Honduras, which was also inhabited by Mayan peoples. Shortly after his arrival in 1524, Olid did exactly what Cortes had done with Velazquez: He declared his independence and went his own way.

Like Velazquez, Cortes sent a force after Olid. But in this case it was Cortes himself who led it. He took along Cuauhtemoc to prevent the Aztecs from rebelling in his absence. When Cortes was informed that the chief was plotting against him, Cuauhtemoc was hanged.

For nearly two years Cortes traveled the swamps and jungles of Honduras. Many of his men died from disease; Cortes himself received a head wound. When he finally caught up with Olid, he discovered that one of his officers had already arrived. Olid was dead.

Cortes returned to Mexico City, but in his absence new rivals had been plotting against him, fearful and jealous of the power and glory he had obtained. So in March 1528, Cortes sailed to Spain to see the king and ask to be named viceroy of New Spain. Cortes had communicated with the king on many occasions, especially in an earlier series of letters explaining his plans for conquering the Aztecs. But it was Cortes's misfortune that this king, Charles V, was not merely king of Spain. He had become the Holy Roman Emperor in 1519 and now ruled most of Europe. Charles had little time for far-distant colonies, except as they contributed to his treasury.

Cortes returned to Spain in triumphant style with a treasure of fine gold and exotic animals such as armadillos. He also brought Native Americans from Mexico. He went back to Mexico in July 1530 with an aristocratic new wife, Juana de Zuniga. His first wife had died some time earlier. Cortes also had a new title, Marquis of the Valley of Oaxaca, but he was not named viceroy.

In 1535 Charles V did name a viceroy of Mexico, Don Antonio de Mendoza. Now outranked in the empire he had hoped to rule, Cortes retired to his estates at Cuernavaca, about 30 miles (48 kilometers) south of Mexico City. From there, he concentrated on more exploration. That year he explored La Paz in Baja California, which he called Santa Cruz and claimed for Spain.

The foundations of a building stand in the ruins of the Aztec city, Tenochtitlan, in present-day Mexico City.

Returning to Spain in 1540 with his sons Martin and Luis, he was injured in a fight against Algiers pirates. Disillusioned and heartsick at his fall from power, Cortes spent the rest of his life writing letters to the king requesting the honors that he felt were his. Cortes died at Castilleja de la Cuesta outside of Seville on December 2, 1547. He was 63 years old. At his request, he was buried in Mexico City.

On the list of Spain's conquistadors, no one achieved more in so short a time than Hernan Cortes. Yet his achievements are forever overshadowed by the brutality that resulted in so great a loss of life to the native peoples of Mexico. He had changed the course of Mexican history forever.

What Did They Find?

The story of early exploration in Central America, Mexico, and the Caribbean is the story of Spanish power in the New World. Like explorers before and since, the conquistadors ruthlessly sought gold, power, and status in the Americas. But Spain, more than the other European nations, was also very concerned with moral problems involving what they looked upon as heathen peoples. Along with men such as Hernan Cortes went Dominican and Franciscan friars who tried to convert the native peoples, with varying degrees of success. They also sometimes tried to protect them from those who had conquered their lands.

From its many expeditions sent to the Americas in the 1400s and 1500s, Spain acquired vast amounts of gold, silver, and other precious gems. But very little of this great wealth ended up being invested in the economic production of the country. Most of it was lavished on the Spanish ruling court and other high officials. A good deal paid for Spanish armies and the seemingly endless wars with Spain's neighbors. Strangely enough, even at the height of its material success in the New World, Spain was a relatively poor country.

The explorers who sailed for Spain during this period present a romanticized picture of the adventurous hero. They braved all dangers and went where no European had gone before. They were certainly great adventurers, brave enough to step into a world they knew very little about. They were sometimes kind but more often brutal in their treatment of the native peoples they encountered. They believed they were sailing for the glory of Spain, but just as often they sought their own glory. However history views these bold mariners, the fact is that they greatly changed the world of their time and ours. For better or for worse, Central America, Mexico, and the Caribbean are forever a product of men such as Columbus and Cortes.

Important Events in the Exploration of Central America, Mexico, and the Caribbean

1492   August 3, Columbus sails from Spain
        October 12, Columbus sights land at the Bahamas
        November 21, Martin Pinzon suddenly leaves the fleet to search for gold
        December 6, Columbus lands at Haiti, which he names Hispaniola

1493   January, Pinzon rejoins Columbus
        March, Columbus returns to Portugal and then Spain
        March 20, Martin Pinzon dies
        September 25, Columbus leaves on second voyage

1494   June 11, Columbus returns to Cadiz

1498   May 30, Columbus leaves Sanlucar on third voyage
        July 31, Columbus lands at Trinidad

1500   November, Columbus returns to Spain in chains

1501   September, Columbus is absolved of all wrongdoing

1502   May 9, fourth voyage of Columbus
        July, Columbus reaches Jamaica

1503   February, Columbus tries settlement in Panama, abandons it in April
        June, Columbus stranded in Jamaica

1504   November 7, Columbus returns to Sanlucar

1508   Vicente Pinzon sails along the coast of Central America

1509   Balboa founds colony of Darien, Panama

1510   Velazquez is named governor of Cuba; Cortes sails with him

1513   September 25, Balboa is first European to see the Pacific from the east

1517   Cordoba explores the Yucatan

1518   Grijalva explores Mexico; Velazquez sends Cortes after him

1519   January, Balboa beheaded for treason; Velazquez sends Narvaez after Cortes
        Easter Sunday, Cortes meets ambassadors of Montezuma
        August 15, Cortes begins march to Tenochtitlan

1520   Cortes defeats Narvaez
        June, Montezuma is killed by his own people
        June 30, Noche Triste, the night during which Cortes loses most of his army

1521   Cuauhtemoc surrenders to Cortes

1522   October 22, Cortes is named governor and captain general of New Spain

1528   March, Cortes sails for Spain

1530   Cortes returns to Mexico without title of viceroy

Glossary

armada large group or fleet of ships

arthritis disease causing inflammation and stiffening of joints

bureaucrat government official who follows a rigid formal routine

caravel small 15th- or 16th-century sailing ship with broad bows and usually three masts

emissary one sent on a mission as an agent, for instance, of the crown

flagship the finest ship in a fleet, usually carrying the group's commander

hieroglyphic system of writing using pictures as script

illusion a misleading image

incense material that produces a fragrant odor when burned

indentured servant person who signs an agreement to work as a servant for a length of time, usually in return for travel expenses

isthmus narrow strip of land connecting two larger areas

knot speed of one nautical mile per hour

loot goods usually seized by violence, as in a war

malaria disease characterized by periodic attacks of chills and fever

mariner one who navigates or assists in the navigation of a ship

mutiny revolt, usually by naval crew, against authority

massacre act of killing a large number of usually defenseless people or animals

peninsula land nearly surrounded by water and connected to land by an isthmus

shackles a restraint, usually metal, that confines the arms and/or legs

smallpox acute contagious disease caused by a virus and characterized by skin eruptions

strait comparatively narrow passageway connecting two large bodies of water

Further Reading

Bohlander, Richard E. (ed.). *World Explorers and Discoverers*. Cambridge, Mass.: Da Capo, 2003.

Baker, Daniel B. (ed.). *Explorers and Discovers of the World*. Detroit: Gale, 1993.

January, Brendan. *Hernan Cortes*. Chicago: Heinemann Library, 2003.

Molzahn, Arlene Bourgeois. *Christopher Columbus: Famous Explorer*. Berkeley Heights, N.J.: Enslow, 2003.

Molzahn, Arlene Bourgeois. *Vasco Nuñez de Balboa: Explorer to the Pacific Ocean*. Berkeley Heights, N.J.: Enslow, 2003.

Pancella, Peggy. *Christopher Columbus*. Chicago: Heinemann Library, 2003.

Index